F-15 Eagle

F-15 Eagle

Roy Braybrook

CRESCENT BOOKS

New York

This 1991 edition published by Crescent Books, distributed by Outlet Book Company, a Random House Company, 225 Park Avenue South, New York, New York 10003.

Printed and bound in Hong Kong

ISBN 0 517 05873 1

87654321

Edited by Tony Holmes
Designed by Paul Kime

Front cover Two F-15As from the 1st Tactical Fighter Training Squadron (TFTS), pictured landing at Luke AFB in 1984. The closer of the two is serialled 74–0119 and the badge on its intake is that of the 325th Tactical Training Wing (TTW) (*Bob Archer*)

Back cover Flight refuelling for this F-15C from the 36th TFW at Bitburg AB (tail-code 'BT') is about to be provided by a KC-135R from the 384th Air Refuelling Sqn, this contact taking place somewhere over the North Sea in 1987. The tanker unit forms a large part of the 384th Bomb Wing, which is in turn part of the 8th Air Force (SAC), headquartered at Barksdale AFB, Louisiana. The wing has about 14 KC-135Rs, which are now primarily tasked with supporting the Rockwell B-1Bs of the 28th BS (*Duncan Cubitt/Airforces Monthly*)

Half title page A standard production F-15J of Japan's *Koku Jieitai* (Air Self-Defense Force), photographed at Komatsu AB on Honshu Island in 1987. This example is part of 306 *Hikotai* (Sqn) of 6 *Kokudan* (Wing), which is one of the units responsible for air defence in the central region (*Peter R Foster*)

Title page Close-up view of an F-15C from the 36th TFW, based at Bitburg AB in southern Germany, refuelling over the North Sea in 1987 from a Boeing KC-135R tanker flown by the 384th Air Refuelling Sqn from McConnell AFB in Kansas (*Duncan Cubitt/Airforces Monthly*)

Contents

Frontline – European Eagles   6

Interceptor America   42

The Guard   76

Strike Fighter   92

Samurai Warrior   100

The Desert Storm   118

Right A pristine F-15C from the 33rd TFW, photographed under stormy skies at the 1990 Battle of Britain Airshow held at Boscombe Down. Usually based at Eglin in Florida, the 33rd sent 12 Eagles (10 C-models and two Ds) to Soesterburg AFB in Holland for exercise *Coronet Trigger*, the wing being generously hosted during the deployment by the resident 32nd TFS (*Tony Holmes*)

Frontline – European Eagles

For the United States Air Force, what matters above all else is control of the air, with absolute certainty above the nation's ground forces, and hopefully far into enemy territory. Given that control, the US Army can proceed with the land battle free from harassment by hostile aircraft, while the USAF can support ground forces both in the battle area and by striking far beyond, interdicting supplies and destroying facilities essential to the enemy war effort. If ever the USAF were to be deprived of that control, the whole game-plan might come unglued.

To achieve that supremacy in the air demands far more than having a slight edge over any potential adversary. The USAF fighters must be able to produce a high exchange-ratio even when significantly outnumbered. Difficult as this undoubtedly is, it is possible through superior training in combination with superior technology. The right equipment will allow the USAF pilot to detect and identify enemy aircraft at extreme range, to engage several of them before they have the opportunity to return fire, and successfully dogfight with the remainder, benefitting from a combat persistence that cannot be achieved in lightweight fighters. The right training will allow that pilot to exploit the potential of the equipment to the maximum.

The key to USAF dominance in the air battle is the McDonnell Douglas F-15 Eagle, today the world's finest ground-based day/night all-weather air superiority fighter. As the USAF's leading combat aircraft, the F-15 might fairly be described as the modern equivalent of the P-51 Mustang that ran up astronomical kill-ratios against German fighters in the closing days of World War 2, and of the F-86 Sabre that beat the MiG-15 by a 10 to 1 ratio in Korea.

Nowhere has the supremacy of the F-15 been more important than in Central Europe where throughout the 1980s NATO forces faced the threat of possible attack by the Warsaw Pact, using the latest and best of Soviet aircraft and SAM (surface-to-air missile) systems. If that attack had come the F-15 would probably have been the first Western aircraft involved. There appears to have been an agreement within NATO – evidently signed at a time when the Germans were felt to be much too enthusiastic about killing Russians – that intruding aircraft from the East would be intercepted first by the USAFE or the RAF.

It was on this basis that on 4 July 1989 a Polish-based MiG-23 *Flogger*, from which the Soviet Air Force pilot had ejected due to engine problems, was intercepted by two USAFE F-15s while on a westerly heading at 37,000 ft

Right This air-to-air shot of F-15D (serial 79–0004) from the 32nd TFS 'Wolfhounds' at Soesterberg AB in the Netherlands, emphasizes the massive wing area of the Eagle, and the use of two light greys in its highly effective countershaded camouflage scheme, ideal for the medium/high level air superiority role (*Ian Black*)

(11,300 m) and 400 knots (740 km/hr), near Osnabruck in what was then West Germany. Since this *Flogger* was pilotless, it was left hopefully to continue out to sea, but unfortunately it ran out of fuel and crashed in Belgium.

The F-15s that performed this intercept came from the 32nd Tactical Fighter Squadron (TFS), based at Soesterberg AB in the Netherlands. However, the principal F-15 unit in Europe is the 36th Tactical Fighter Wing (TFW) at Bitburg in southern Germany. The 32nd TFS and the 36th TFW are components of the 17th Air Force (USAFE), headquartered at Sembach AB.

Above Returning from a BFM (Basic Fighting Manoeuvres) sortie which has seen the pair of Eagles scrapping with a pair of diminutive Hawks, the mixed formation banks towards Decimomannu, in Sardinia. Both F-15Ds are crewed by 'novice' fighter pilots recently posted to the 32nd TFS, this particular sortie aimed at increasing the 'freshman's' familiarity with his aircraft in a combat environment. This photograph graphically illustrates the varying sizes of modern fighter aircraft, the Eagle being far easier to spot than the diminutive Hawk (*Ian Black*)

Left An unusual combination: two F-15Ds (81–0065 and 79–0004) formating on a British Aerospace Hawk T.Mk 1A trainer from the RAF's No 2 Tactical Weapons Unit (No 63 'Shadow' Sqn) at Chivenor. The Hawk is painted in a darker shade of grey, reflecting its low-level airfield defence war-role (*Ian Black*)

A fine study of F-15C serial 79–0031, assigned to the 32nd TFS, about to touch down at Schleswig-Jagel in Northern Germany, the principal *Bundesmarine* airbase. Eagles of the 32nd TFS are identified by the 'CR' tail-code and orange fin-stripe outlined in green (*Bob Archer*)

Left The F-15D seen from above, demonstrating how (as Sea Harrier pilots discovered in the Falklands conflict of 1982) a pale grey camouflage scheme stands out like a sore thumb against the colour of the sea. The glint off the unpainted metal over the afterburners would also act as a beacon to a trained fighter pilot's eye. Due to its huge wing area, the Eagle has been unflatteringly dubbed the 'supersonic tennis court' (*Ian Black*)

Above In side-view there is less to see of the Eagle, since the side-by-side arrangement of the engines results in a shallow rear fuselage, and the use of twin fins reduces the projected area. Radar cross-section benefits accordingly, though it may be noted that the fins are truly vertical (*Ian Black*)

Left Close-up of F-15C 79–0018, clearly taken from a tanker, and emphasizing the fine lines of the Hughes APG-63 radome (*Peter R Foster*)

Above Two F-15Cs of the 32nd TFS in deployment configuration, each with three 500 Imp gal (2275 litre) tanks. The carriage of two AIM-9 Sidewinders on the stub-pylons appears to be general practice for Eagle squadrons (*Peter R Foster*)

Left Another Eagle from the 32nd TFS smokes skyward. Powered by two Pratt & Whitney F100-PW-220 turbofans, each with a static thrust of 23,770 lbs (10,780 kgs), the F-15C is probably burning fuel at around 1750 lbs/min (800 kg/min) at this stage. At 600 knots (1110 km/hr) at sea level, the aircraft is getting lighter at 2500 lbs/min (1130 kgs/min). Closing rapidly on the departing F-15 are a pair of Lightning F.6s, the RAF's ultimate British interceptor. This shot was taken at RAF Binbrook in the early 1980s, the base having since been closed (*Ian Black*)

Below Two Soesterberg Eagles arrive at RAF Alconbury in early 1987 for dissimilar air combat training (DACT) with the F-5Es of the 527th TFT Aggressor Sqn. The aircraft behind 81–0046 is 79–0032, the last two digits of its serial forming the 32 TFS marking on its tail, and with the 'Wolfhound' paint-job on the front fuselage (*Bob Archer*)

Left The Eagle at sunset. This rear-end view of the F-15C illustrates the close proximity of the two engines, a design factor which suggests that major damage to one powerplant could also affect the other. The bolt-upright tail surfaces are also noteworthy, especially when you consider that present-day stealth-conscious designers tend to incline the fins to reduce lateral radar response (*Ian Black*)

Above An all-too-rare example of unit artwork on the front fuselage of F-15C 79–0032. Assigned to flight commander Major Bob 'Laser' Stratton, this F-15 is liberally stencilled with the technical graffiti that adorns all modern combat aircraft. The 32nd TFS combine a comic wolf's head with the royal Dutch crest as their unit insignia (*Ian Black*)

Left Flt Lt Steve Bridger of No 11 Sqn (then equipped with Lightnings) ascends to the cockpit of F-15D serial 79–0004 for a familiarization sortie during a 32nd TFS detachment to RAF Binbrook in late 1986 (*T Malcolm English*)

Below Bridger settles down in the rear cockpit, while his pilot, Capt Allee, is strapped down to the front 'bang-seat'. An interesting detail of this photograph is the telescopic sight, taken from a rifle and bolted to the Head-Up Display (HUD), to assist in long-range target recognition (*T Malcolm English*)

Below Even a 'Wolfhound' has to rest sometimes. The fading light makes this F-15C appear tatty, but the aircraft is painted in the standard USAF countershaded scheme combining what is officially termed as high and low reflectance 'gray'. For the technically-minded, the colours are Dark Compass Ghost Grey (Federal Standard 595a–36320) and Light Compass Ghost Grey (FS595a–36375) (*Ian Black*)

Left This rear-aspect view of the same aircraft (79–0032) shows that, even for a modern fighter, quite a lot of light can be reflected from its surface. From this viewpoint the ideal paint finish would be matt (or 'lustreless' in US terminology), but this results in a surface that is easily contaminated and an aircraft that soon loses its smart appearance. As a compromise most current combat aircraft (including this F-15C) have a semi-gloss finish (*Ian Black*)

Right I think this Eagle is winking at me! The drooping intakes go asymmetric as the engines are started, once again at RAF Binbrook. Eagles were first deployed to Soesterberg (or Camp New Amsterdam) in 1975 and have subsequently demonstrated some remarkable sortie-generation rates.

In an exercise named *Maximum Push* (16–25 July 1979) 15 Eagles generated 442 sorties totalling 521 flight hours. The squadron attained a full mission-capable rate of 74 per cent and the groundcrews were able to supply more fighters than there were pilots available (*T Malcolm English*)

Below A pleasing shot of 32nd TFS Eagles on the flight-line at RAF Binbrook during a 1986 deployment. The F-15 must have provided an interesting contrast with that station's Lightnings, which, although

capable of a useful climb rate and ceiling, were designed on the traditional RAF 'straight-up and straight-down' philosophy, with internal fuel to match (*T Malcolm English*)

Left The Eagle's flight refuelling receptacle is open, the boom of the KC-135R is aimed at it and insertion is about to take place. The USAF has developed the 'flying-boom' refuelling system rather than the hose, drogue and probe concept adopted by the US Navy and the British services, primarily because only the large-diameter boom can provide the high fuel flow rates required by SAC bombers
(*Duncan Cubitt/Airforces Monthly*)

Above Contact is made. This wider-angle shot over the boom-operator's shoulder, with the Eagle generating some bank angle, was taken in 1979 over what was then West Germany. In those days the 36th TFW had F-15As (this example, 76–0008, is currently in storage pending transfer to an ANG unit). Interestingly, the tanker (59–1504) is a KC-135Q from the 349th ARS, which is part of the 9th Strategic Reconnaissance Wing at Beale AFB, California, in turn part of the 15th Air Force (SAC), headquartered at March AFB in the same state
(*T Malcolm English*)

Above Fighters come in all sizes! This Bitburg-based F-15C (80–0025) was photographed in 1982 during a DACT sortie over the North Sea with an F-5E Tiger II (74–01542) from the 527th TFT Aggressor Sqn at RAF Alconbury. The F-5E is wearing one of the many different paint schemes that were applied to the instructors' aircraft to heighten the realism of the combat training provided by the unit (*T Malcolm English*)

Right One Bitburg Eagle making like a homesick angel. The red stripe on the fin of F-15C 80–0003 indicates that this aircraft flies with the 22nd TFS. As the principal F-15 wing in a frontline location, the 36th TFW is expected to attain the highest standards. During a war-readiness surge exercise on 13 September 1978, 71 Eagles generated 322 sorties and 256.8 flight hours in only 22.8 hours of elapsed time. Full mission-capable rate was a remarkable 94 per cent at the start, but was still a highly respectable 75 per cent at the end of the test, which was flown in bad weather with only one runway operational (*David Donald*)

Above Another F-15C from the 22nd TFS, serial 79–0057, performing what is sometimes termed a 'garbage roll' (landing gear down) at a display at RAF Mildenhall in 1987. From a technical viewpoint, this photograph brings out the son-of-Phantom II wing planform, the dogtooth leading edge of the horizontal stabilizer and the typically McDonnell lateral booms alongside the engines, which carry the four tail surfaces (*Bob Archer*)

Above right A pleasing view of F-15C 84–0006 coming in to land at RAF Lakenheath in 1989. The yellow stripe at the tip of the fin indicates that the aircraft is assigned to the 53rd TFS at Bitburg. A TAC fighter wing has a nominal establishment of 72 aircraft, forming three 24-aircraft squadrons, but current reference works indicate that the 36th TFW has about 69 F-15Cs and 7 F-15Ds (*Bob Archer*)

Below right These Bitburg Eagles are about to land at RAF Alconbury in 1981. Their serials are 79–0062 and –0045 and the blue fin stripe indicates assignment to the 525th TFS. The Eagle's airbrake is probably one of the most effective in the business, but it has been criticized for its effect on rear view in combat. The original airbrake design produced severe buffet at 60-degrees extension so it was rehashed and the travel limited to 45 degrees (*Robbie Shaw*)

Another F-15C (84–0003) from the 22nd TFS, this time taxying past during an airshow at RAF Alconbury in 1982. The addition of a unit insignia on the black band on the inner surface of the vertical tail is noteworthy, as is the carriage of a centreline 500 Imp Gal (2275 litre) tank which appears to be virtually standard practice amongst F-15 units *(Duncan Cubitt/Airforces Monthly)*

This study of the front fuselage of a 36th TFW F-15C illustrates how high the pilot sits in the cockpit (exposed virtually from the waist up), the massive teardrop canopy providing him with an excellent 360° field of vision. Also visible from this angle is the sharp-edged engine intake, this design featuring an important innovation which allows it to be rotated about the lower lip to match the capture area to the demands of the engine. Relative to the datum position, it can be drooped through eleven degrees and raised through four degrees (*Ian Black*)

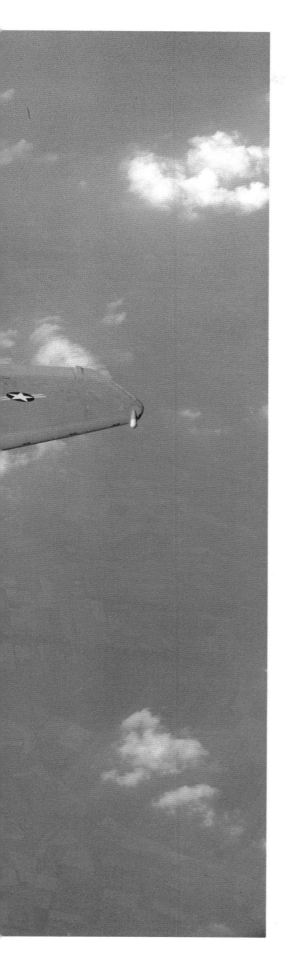

Below At first sight the idea of simulated combat between an F-15C and an F-5E may appear absurd, since the Eagle can blow the Tiger away in a beyond-visual-range engagement. However, in close combat a well-flown F-5E, which is highly manoeuvrable and difficult to see, can give the F-15 a hard time. In the course of air intercept missile evaluation (AIMVAL) trials in the late 1970s, F-15s initially produced excellent exchange ratios against the F-5E by using their radar to position behind the simply-equipped Northrop aircraft. Then the pilots of the F-5Es bought radar-warning devices from car equipment shops and the kill-ratio changed drastically! (*T Malcolm English*)

Left Another flight refuelling portrait of the Eagle, this old F-15A (76–0061) from the 36th TFW closing in on the KC-135Q with receptacle open over the North Sea in 1979. This aircraft now holds the dubious distinction of being the oldest airframe currently assigned to the 48th Fighter Interceptor Squadron (FIS) at Langley AFB, Virginia (*T Malcolm English*)

Below This F-15C from the 22nd TFS at Bitburg (serial 79–0051) was photographed at RAF Wyton in 1983. The small coloured 'star-and-bars' on the front fuselage is typical of the style of national insignia worn by USAFE units throughout the early 1980s, low-viz coming into vogue later in the decade. The intake insignia consists of the highly stylized 36th TFW crest which is worn by all wing F-15s. Most Bitburg Eagles now wear the crest on the right intake, the individual unit emblem taking pride of place on the left side (*Bob Archer*)

Right The pilot of a 36th TFW F-15C, strapped down to his McDonnell Douglas ACES II ejection seat, prepares to go up there and draw a bead on the enemy with his McDonnell Douglas Electronics AVQ-20 head-up display (HUD). In 'gun' mode, the radar provides on the HUD a target designator box to assist in visual acquisition and feeds target range information to the fire control computer. The pilot is presented with a highly accurate aiming mark and a digital read-out of how many rounds of ammunition remain from the original 940 (*Ian Black*)

Below Taxying around the perimeter at RAF Alconbury, this 36th TFW F-15C (79–0044) bears a blue fin stripe, thus denoting it as being a member of the 525th TFS. At low rpm the intakes appear to droop to the minimum capture position, although this facility was developed primarily to reduce spill drag and minimize the adverse effect on directional stability at high angle-of-attack (AOA) (*Robbie Shaw/Pictorial Press*)

Left Close-up of the muzzle of the General Electric M61A1 Gatling of the 36th TFW's F-15A 76–0046, pictured in 1979. The Eagle was originally to have been armed with a new Philco-Ford GAU-7/A cannon, firing caseless ammunition. However, this ran into problems with ammunition storage and uneven propellant burning, so the F-15 reverted to the trusty old 20 mm six-barrel M61 Vulcan, which had entered service with the F-104 and F-105 from 1958. Nominal cyclic rate is 6000 rd/min, although up to 7200 rd/min can be achieved (*T Malcolm English*)

Above An interesting example of toned-down markings on the tail of F-15D 84–0043 of the 53rd TFS, 36th TFW, photographed at Mildenhall in 1989. The two upper excrescences on the trailing edge of the fins house radar-warning receivers for the Loral ALR-56C system, a further two aerials being faired into the wing tips of the aircraft to give the Eagle a full 360° coverage. The larger bullet fairing atop the port fin houses polarized jammers for the Northrop ALQ-135(V) countermeasures set, as do the small 'warts' at the end of each tailboom. Returning to the twin fins, the smaller fairings beneath the RWRs contain a white navigation light on the port side and a red anti-collision beacon on the starboard side (*T Malcolm English*)

Right This brightly-painted F-15B (71–0291), then known as a TF-15A, appeared in its bicentennial markings at Farnborough in 1976 (*T Malcolm English*)

Interceptor America

Providing effective air defence for the continental US (CONUS) is clearly high on the list of USAF priorities. The possibility of attacks by large numbers of Soviet bombers has admittedly receded, but strikes by small numbers of flight-refuelled aircraft that can launch cruise missiles remains a threat, as does the concept of an attempted air attack (naturally on a very limited scale) from a still-hostile Cuba.

Aerospace Defense Command disappeared some years ago, but several CONUS-based active duty and Air National Guard (ANG) units are still assigned to air defence, while the monitoring of satellites and the interception of intercontinental ballistic missiles is now the responsibility of Air Force Space Command (AFSPACECOM).

Air sovereignty and air defence of the CONUS area is the brief of the commander of the 1st Air Force (TAC), headquartered at Langley AFB, Virginia. There have in recent years been three Eagle-equipped fighter interceptor squadrons dedicated to CONUS air defence: the 5th FIS at Minot AFB, North Dakota; the 48th FIS at Langley AFB, Virginia; and the 318th FIS at McChord AFB in Washington state. In addition, the F-15s of the 21st TFW at Elmendorf AFB, which is part of Alaskan Air Command (AAC), is charged with strategic air defence, as is the 57th FIS at Keflavik Naval Air Station (NAS), Iceland. As part of Air Forces Iceland, the 57th comes under 1st Air Force (TAC) control.

Almost traditionally, CONUS air defence has been the task of the delta-winged Convair (GD) F-106 Delta Dart, augmented in recent years by the F-4E Phantom II. However, by the mid-1980s both of these aircraft had grown old, fallen behind in performance and were costing a great deal to operate.

The F-15, having one of the highest thrust to weight ratios currently available and a comparatively modest wing loading, offered the prospect of an extremely high climb rate and an outstanding ceiling. Further, it has a far more advanced radar than either the F-106 or the F-4E, and can carry the Hughes/Raytheon AIM-120 AMRAAM missile (AIM-7 Sparrow-replacement), allowing the simultaneous engagement of multiple beyond-visual-range (BVR) targets.

Having first flown on 27 July 1972, the F-15 literally 'zoomed' through its development programme, establishing a series of eight world records for

Left Production of the F-15A/B began with FY73 funding, and the first unit to be Eagle-equipped was the 1st TFW (tail-code 'FF') at Langley AFB. This line-up of F-15As was recorded in 1980, the red stripes on their fins confirming that all five were assigned to 71st TFS, as indicated by the tail-marking of 76–0071 in the distance. This particular airframe is the squadron commander's personal mount, and it bears a deluxe version of the standard fin-stripe. The badge visible on the left intake of all five aircraft is that of the 1st TFW (*Steve Hill via Bob Archer*)

time-to-height by 1975, shattering earlier figures set by the F-4 and MiG-25 Foxbat in the process. To quote just two examples from this Project *Streak Eagle*, the F-15's time to 49,000 ft (15,000 m) was 77.04 seconds from wheels-rolling, compared to 114.50 seconds for the F-4, and twice that height was reached in 207.80 seconds by the F-15, compared to 243.86 seconds by the MiG-25. These performances clearly demonstrated the Eagle's potential in the high altitude intercept role.

Aside from the units mentioned in the context of dedicated interception, the F-15 equips several other US-based active duty wings. These are the 1st TFW at Langley and the 33rd TFW at Eglin AFB, both based in Florida and both coming within the jurisdiction of the 9th Air Force (TAC), and the 49th TFW at Holloman AFB, New Mexico, which is part of the 12th Air Force (TAC), 833rd Air Division. The F-15 is also employed by numerous training and test establishments.

Above The Eagle is seen so frequently with only its lightweight AIM-9Ls in place that it may be forgotten that in war it carries four medium-range AIM-7 Sparrows for BVR engagements. This example, displayed alongside a 1st TFW F-15C at an open-day at NAS Norfolk, Virginia, appears to be temporarily short of wings, but these were undoubtedly about to be added. Like its famous forebear the F-4, the F-15 carries four AIM-7s semi-recessed for low drag.

Aside from its old technology, the AIM-7 operates on semi-active radar homing which requires the launch aircraft to continue illuminating the target throughout missile flight, involving the risk of return fire by even short-range missiles. Its AIM-120 AMRAAM replacement is a fire-and-forget weapon with active radar terminal homing that will allow the F-15 to engage several targets simultaneously (*Peter R Foster*)

Right This photograph of an F-15C from the 94th TFS/1st TFW was taken during a deployment to RAF Waddington for a Tactical Fighter Meet in 1988. The

squadron's aircraft are identified by a blue fin stripe, a feature not visible in this centre-line view (*T Malcolm English*)

Left In stark contrast to the flat countryside of Alconbury, this 1st TFW Eagle has as its backdrop the mountains of Nevada. It was photographed taxying in after a Red Flag sortie in 1987 (*Frank B Mormillo*)

Above One snowy Eagle at RAF Alconbury in January 1979. The 'FF' tail-code and yellow fin band mark this as a refugee from the 27th TFS/1st TFW, and the serial 74–0132 confirms that it is a very early production F-15A. Long since replaced at Langley by a more modern F-15C, this particular aircraft is now abused on a daily basis by 'green' Eagle drivers under instruction with the 325th Tactical Training Wing (TTW) at Tyndall AFB. (*Bob Archer*)

Above left More F-15As of the 71st/TFS 1st
TFW, lined up on the Langley concrete in
1980. The wing is earmarked for overseas
assignments with the Rapid Deployment
Force (as in the case of the 1990 Gulf crisis),
but also has commitments in regard to the
air defence of the eastern seaboard
(*Steve Hill*)

Below left Possibly the world's most
expensive gate-guard, this F-15A (71–0281)
was photographed at the main gates of
Langley AFB in 1988. First flown on 26
September 1972, this particular aircraft was
the second of 12 prototypes built for the
Eagle programme. During its flying career
with the USAF, '0281 was responsible for
testing the Pratt & Whitney F100–PW-100
engines. Langley is the second oldest
continuously active air base in the US, and
was named after the aviation pioneer
Samuel Pierpoint Langley, who died in
1906. It accommodates the headquarters of
TAC, and thus has an outstanding officers'
club, of which this author was an honorary
member while on loan to the NASA
Langley Research Center some years ago!
The wind tunnels and other test facilities
are on the other side of the airfield from the
USAF base (*Paul Bigelow via Bob Archer*)

Above This F-15C from the 21st TFW, based
at Elmendorf AFB, Alaska, is shown taking
off from Nellis AFB, in Nevada, during the
course of a Red Flag training exercise. It
bears the unit's 'AK' tail-code, but no fin-
stripe to associate it with either of the
wing's two squadrons (*Frank B Mormillo*)

Above These two F-15Cs landing at Elmendorf AFB (serials 78–0546 and 81–0020) bear the yellow fin stripe of the 54th TFS. The Plough constellation painted on the black inboard fin stripe is the wing badge, derived from the Alaskan Air Command insignia (*Peter R Foster*)

Right The 21st TFW has only 34 Eagles, which form two squadrons. The 43rd TFS is distinguished by a blue fin stripe, as in the case of this F-15C (80–0018) pictured taxying at Elmendorf in 1989. The shield painted on the fin is the winged star and Plough constellation of AAC (*Peter R Foster*)

Left The Eglin-based Eagles of the 33rd TFW bear an 'EG' tail-code and are operated as three squadrons; the 58th TFS with a blue fin stripe; the 59th TFS ('Golden Pride') with a yellow fin stripe; and the 60th ('Fighting Crows') TFS with a red fin stripe. The wing traces its origins back to the 33rd Pursuit Group, which flew Curtiss P-40s before Pearl Harbor. Assigned to the 60th TFS, F-15D 85–0132 was one of four 'Fighting Crows' Eagles that turned up at the 1990 Battle of Britain Airshow held at Boscombe Down in Hampshire (*Tony Holmes*)

Above Another visitor to Boscombe Down was F-15D 85-0134, also assigned to the 60th TFS. As with many Eagle operators, the 33rd TFW have adorned the inside of each fin with a highly stylized bird of prey. Eglin, located in Florida just south-west of the twin cities of Niceville and Valparaiso, forms (with Hurlburt Field) by far the largest airbase in the western world. It was set up in the 1930s as a gunnery and bombing facility, and the host unit is still the Munitions Systems Division which includes the 3246th Test Wing. Other tenants include the Tactical Air Warfare Center, which mounts Blue Flag and Green Flag exercises, and the 39th Special Operations Wing. The base was named after Lt Col Frederick I Eglin, a World War I aviator who died in a flying accident in 1937 (*Tony Holmes*)

This pair of F-15As from the 49th TFW (tail-code 'HO') represent two squadrons. On the right, 77–0140 has a blue fin-stripe, indicating the 7th TFS, while on the left 77–0127 has a yellow stripe for the 8th TFS. They were photographed on a visit to Tyndall AFB from their home-base of Holloman AFB in New Mexico during 1982.

The 49th shares the base with the 479th TTW, which is the other major component of the 833rd Air Division of the 12th Air Force (TAC). The base was named after Col George Holloman, a pioneer in guided weaponry, who was killed in a B-17 crash on Formosa in 1946 (*Bob Archer*)

Rear-quarter view of the same pair of F-15As, illustrating the minimal smoke emission of the Eagle, far less than in the case of its Phantom II ancestor. The 49th has shown up extremely well in readiness exercises. In the course of one inspection lasting three days in April 1979, some 48 Eagles generated 428 sorties and 469 flight hours, and demonstrated a full mission-capable rate of 80 per cent. Average scramble time was 3 minutes 42 seconds (*Bob Archer*)

Left One of Holloman's Eagles, seen over the Mojave Desert in southern California. Serialled 77–0086, its red fin-stripe indicates the 9th TFS. The open refuelling receptacle suggests it was photographed from a tanker, and the black wing stripes may be explained by the fact that it was taking part in a Lobo Flag '88 exercise. The 49th TFW has the distinction of being the only frontline Eagle Wing equipped entirely with the old F-15A (*Frank B Mormillo*)

Above As shown here, Nellis AFB in Nevada provides some spectacular scenery, but it also serves as home for the 57th Fighter Weapons Wing (tail-code 'WA'). The aircraft in this 1981 photograph is an F-15A (75–0055), wearing on its intake the unit's badge, a sheaf of red arrows striking the bulls-eye of a black and yellow target (*Denis J Calvert*)

Left That same aircraft, complete with early white tail-codes, is seen taxying in after a Red Flag sortie in November 1978. The wing's Eagles bear a black and yellow chequered fin-stripe, and are operated by the 422nd TFS. The 57th FWW operates many other types of aircraft, such as the A-10, F-16 and F-111, and its components include the USAF Demonstration Sqn ('Thunderbirds'), which currently flies F-16s. Nellis AFB was established in 1947 and was named after 1st Lt William H Nellis, a World War 2 P-47 pilot who was killed in late 1944 in Europe (*T Malcolm English*)

Above One of the components of the 57th FWW is the 433rd FWS, exemplified by this pair of F-15Bs (77–0164 and –0162). The squadron badge on the black fin stripe makes an unusual change from the more typical Eagle design
(*USAF official via Bob Archer*)

Below Some bizarre paint schemes have been tried out in the course of camouflage development, as demonstrated by this F-15B (then termed a TF-15A). Part of the then Eagle-equipped 58th TTW based at Luke AFB in Arizona, this aircraft (74–0139) wore the Keith Ferris splinter scheme for most of 1977 as part of a USAF/US Navy evaluation of tactical colours. As with Canadian Hornets, this Eagle wears a false canopy on the undersurface of the forward fuselage. The 58th TTW now fly various versions of the F-16 Fighting Falcon out of Luke (*Paul Goddard via Bob Archer*)

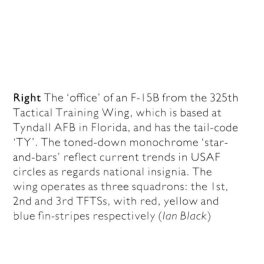

Right The 'office' of an F-15B from the 325th Tactical Training Wing, which is based at Tyndall AFB in Florida, and has the tail-code 'TY'. The toned-down monochrome 'star-and-bars' reflect current trends in USAF circles as regards national insignia. The wing operates as three squadrons: the 1st, 2nd and 3rd TFTSs, with red, yellow and blue fin-stripes respectively (*Ian Black*)

Left White knuckle time! Judging by the patches, this is an RAF exchange pilot on loan to the 1st TFTS, preparing to depart in an aircraft that he might well decide his service should have purchased in place of the air defence variant of the Tornado (*Ian Black*)

Above Chocks away! The F-15B, identified by the intake badge as belonging to the 1st TFTS, prepares for flight. Tyndall AFB was activated at the end of 1941, and was named after 1st Lt Frank B Tyndall, a World War I fighter pilot who died in 1930 when his Curtiss P-1 Hawk crashed (*Ian Black*)

Below An F-15A (74–0126) poses for the camera, its red fin-stripe and unit badge identifying it as a member of the 1st TFTS. The tail feathers of an F-14A from VF-101 'Grim Reapers', a fleet replenishment air group (RAG) unit based at NAS Oceana, Virginia, just creep into the corner of this shot. The students from Tyndall often test their mettle against fellow freshmen from the Tomcat community, as VF-101 maintain a permanent detachment at NAS Key West in Florida (*Ian Black*)

Right The 405th TTW (tail-code 'LA'), based at Luke AFB, Arizona, is part of the 832nd Air Division of the 12th Air Force (TAC). The 405th operates a mix of F-15A/B/D/Es, with the A/Bs forming two squadrons: the 426th TFTS with a red fin-stripe, and the 555th TFTS with a green stripe containing five white stars. These two F-15As from the 405th are seen over the Mojave Desert during a training sortie, which may explain the black squares on the wings of the leading aircraft (*Frank B Mormillo*)

Left The range and endurance of this 405th TTW F-15A are clearly about to be 'Extended'. The H-configuration tail surfaces on the boom identify the tanker as a McDonnell Douglas KC-10 Extender, and the rough terrain below is a sizeable chunk of the Mojave Desert. The tanker is a 10th Air Force AFRES aircraft from the 452nd AREFW, which implies membership of the 79th Air Refuelling Sqn (AFRES), based at March AFB, California. The introduction of the KC-10 brought many improvements relative to the old KC-135, including an increase in fuel flow rate from 750 to 1250 Imp gal (3400 to 5700 litres) per minute. As an alternative to the boom, the KC-10 can deploy a hose and drogue, and two additional hose units are now being added under the wingtips to allow up to three US Navy or NATO aircraft to be refuelled simultaneously. The USAF has purchased a total of 60 KC-10s (*Frank B Mormillo*)

Above Refuelling completed, this F-15A from the 555th TFTS peels away (*Frank B Mormillo*)

Above If the gear sticks in this position, Maj Clif Lopert can always land on the centreline tank! This F-15A (76–0067) of the 555th TFTS is just commencing another training sortie over the parched earth that surrounds Luke AFB. The red light at the leading edge kink is an anti-collision beacon (*David Donald*)

Above right Unlike the Eagles of CONUS-based air defence units, the F-15Cs of the 57th FIS, based at NAS Keflavik in Iceland, carry no fin flashes but a two-letter tail-code (IS). All aircraft of this unit also have a black and white chequered stripe at the top of the fin. The first of 18 Eagles assigned to the 'Black Knights of Keflavik' arrived in October 1985 to begin their task of intercepting Soviet *Bear*, *Badger* and *Bison* aircraft, which penetrate south into the Atlantic via gaps between Greenland and Iceland and between Iceland and the UK. Records show that the 57th intercept more Soviet aircraft than any other USAF unit. This F-15C (80–0038) is seen landing at RAF Alconbury in 1988 (*Bob Archer*)

Below right As exemplified by this F-15A (76–0015) of the 5th FIS, photographed in 1985, the markings of this unit consist of 'gold' (in practice, yellow) lightning bolts with dark-blue edges, but some stars appear to have been added for good measure also. The 5th is based at Minot AFB, North Dakota. This particular aircraft has more recently been reported with the Air Guard's 102nd FIW at Otis ANGB, Massachusetts, indicating that the 5th has replaced it with an F-15C (*Doug Remington via Bob Archer*)

This pair of F-15As (76–0113 and 0104) from the 48th FIS was photographed taking off from Tyndall AFB in 1982, with nosegear doors just closing. The 48th FIS was the first CONUS air defence unit to receive the Eagle, aircraft initially arriving in July 1981, with the squadron completing its conversion from the ageing F-106 early in 1982. Relative to the old Convair Delta Dart, the Eagle provided not only higher performance, but also superior weapons (with the AIM-7, AIM-9 and M61 gun) and the ability to see and track low-flying objects (*Bob Archer*)

Another F-15A (76–0100) of the 48th FIS, this time pictured at home at Langley AFB, Virginia. All USAF air defence units have distinctive markings on their vertical tails. In the case of the 48th, as illustrated here, the basic identifier is the blue and white striped rudder, but all the unit's aircraft also appear to bear a white vee-shaped flash on the fin, outlined in blue. The fin also carries the TAC shield, while unit badges are painted on the intake sides (*Milslides via Bob Archer*)

Above Two generations of USAF interceptors are illustrated by this rainy-day photograph from 1983, marking the delivery of the first F-15B (76–0141) to the 318th FIS at McChord AFB in Washington. In the background sits a tired old F-106A (59–0141), their serials representing a 17-year leap in technology. In reality, the Delta Dart was quite an aircraft for its day, with an internal armament of four AIM-4E/F Super Falcons and a nuclear-tipped AIR-2A/B Genie. The 418th's tail marking is described as a dark blue/light blue star with a white centre containing the unit badge (*Doug Remington via Bob Archer*)

Right An F-15A (76–0008) from the 318th FIS, pictured at Tyndall AFB, Florida, in 1984, during a William Tell Weapons Meet, showing its smart personalized jetpipe plugs (*Don Abrahamson via Bob Archer*)

Left The Air Force Flight Test Center at Edwards AFB, California, (tail-code 'ED') is part of Air Force Systems Command (AFSC). The center has a wide range of aircraft, which are operated by the 6512th Test Operations Sqn, and generally bear a blue fin-stripe with white crosses. This F-15A 77–0139 appears to be a permanent item of equipment (*via Bob Archer*)

Above The fin marking of Edwards aircraft is well illustrated by the tail of F-15B 77–0166, which also bears the insignia of AFSC and the 'Firefly' badge of the integrated fire and flight-control (IFFC) system test. In essence, IFFC allowed the aircraft's radar or other sensors to fly it in an effort to reduce air-to-air and air-to-ground miss distances using guns, rockets and bombs. The aim was to eliminate the effect of human errors in the use of unguided weaponry, but it remains to be seen if such systems will be fitted to the Advanced Tactical Fighter that is planned to replace the Eagle
(*Doug Remington via Bob Archer*)

The Guard

Incredible as it may seem by European (and most other) standards, some early-model Eagles (ie, the F-15A and two-seat F-15B) are now being passed to Air National Guard units, replacing old combat aircraft such as the F-4.

In reality, the ANG is a unique service, not only in terms of its equipment standard (which includes aircraft such as the C-5A Galaxy, KC-135E Stratotanker and F-16A/B Fighting Falcon), but also in terms of the contribution it makes to the total capability of the USAF, and in having state and federal missions.

In peacetime, ANG units are commanded by the governors of their states, and are assigned to appropriate USAF commands (TAC, SAC, MAC or PACAF), which assist in training and readiness programmes. In various emergency situations, any ANG unit may be called to federal active duty, either by the President or by Congress. This can take place not only in the case of invasion or to suppress an insurrection, but also in the event of an overseas conflict. For example, ANG units played major roles in Korea and Vietnam, and ANG A-7s of the 180th Tactical Fighter Group (TFG) from Toledo, Ohio, flew 22 close air support sorties during Operation *Just Cause* when the US invaded Panama in December 1989 to end the rule of General Noriega.

These operational missions represented the culmination of *Coronet Cove*, the ANG's 11-year commitment to defend the Panama Canal. Between December 1978 and the end of January 1990, it is estimated that ANG units, based in rotation at Howard AFB, Panama, had flown 16,959 hours in the course of over 13,000 sorties

To illustrate the contribution made by the ANG to the USAF, by the end of the 1980s the Guard had 115,000 members and was providing 85 per cent of the fighter-interceptor force. It also represented about 60 per cent of the tactical air support effort, 50 per cent of the reconnaissance force, almost 35 per cent of the tactical airlift, 25 per cent of the tactical fighters, 18 per cent of flight refuelling capability, 17 per cent of the SAR, and five per cent of the strategic airlift! The ANG also has 10 aeromedical evacuation facilities, representing 24 per cent of USAF capacity.

Air Guard training sessions often include overseas deployments, and the service's commitments include full-time responsibilities. Thus, the ANG unit in Hawaii (F-15 equipped) is responsible for the air defence of that state, ANG tanker units maintain aircraft on round-the-clock alert, and the ANG shares with the Air Force Reserve (AFRES) the responsibility for tactical airlift support in Central and Southern America.

Right Another view of a 128th TFS Eagle at London. The 116th TFW is based at Dobbins AFB, just south of Marietta, and the field is also used by the 94th Tactical Airlift Wing (AFRES). The base was activated in 1943, and was named after Capt Charles Dobbins, a World War 2 pilot who was killed in action near Sicily (*Robbie Shaw*)

The first ANG unit to receive the F-15A/B was the 122nd TFS of the 159th TFG, based at New Orleans, Louisiana, with deliveries commencing in June 1985. Similar Eagles now equip the 116th TFW at Dobbins AFB, Georgia, and the 199th TFS of the 154th Composite Group at Hickam AFB, Hawaii. They have also been issued to the 102nd FIW at Otis ANGB, Massachusetts, and the 142nd FIG at Portland, Oregon, which are both dedicated air defence units.

Below An informative view of 128th TFS 116th TFW F-15A (75–0058) from the Georgia ANG, seen visiting London, Ontario, for the 1989 airshow. Clearly visible is the ANG badge and the use of the state's name in yellow on a black band with red borders. The blue, yellow, red and green stripes at the base of the rudder indicate that this is the wing commander's mount (*Robbie Shaw*)

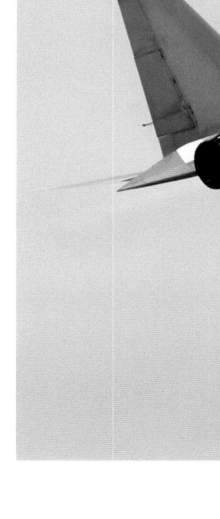

Right What a difference a year can make! Photographed in June 1990, this F-15A (75–0024) illustrates the same unit's introduction of toned-down markings (*Robbie Shaw*)

Left Close-up of the tail feathers of 75–0058, as it appeared in June 1989 (*Robbie Shaw*)

Above Mission completed, a seasoned ANG driver strides away from '0058. The aircraft will now undergo a thorough post sortie check by groundcrew before it is declared operational for its next flight (*Robert F Dorr*)

Previous pages This in-flight photograph of a 122nd TFS F-15A (73–0101) shows the unit markings more clearly, and also the Louisiana ANG insignia. The unit now has 24 F-15As and two F-15Bs, supported by one C-130H Hercules. Eagles of the 159th TFG bear a fin stripe that is blue, green, red or yellow (*Ian Black*)

Above The first Guard unit to receive the Eagle was the 122nd TFS of the 159th TFG of the Louisiana ANG, illustrated here by Maj Steve Decker's F-15A 73–0095. The unit's Eagles (amongst the first ever built for the USAF) were delivered in the summer of 1985, replacing F-4Cs. The 159th is based at NAS New Orleans, some 15 miles (24 km) south of the city. The airfield is also known as Alvin Callender Field, after Alvin A Callender who served with the Royal Flying Corps during World War 1, and died in action over France in 1918 (*Ian Black*)

Right The 199th FIS of the 154th Composite Group is Hawaii's only air defence unit, but it is equipped with two dozen Eagles (and two two-seaters). This F-15A (74–0091), with 74–0086 and others in the background, was photographed at Hickam AFB, the 199th's tropical home. The base was one of the principal targets in the Pearl Harbor raid, and is situated 10 miles (16 km) west of Honolulu. It was activated in 1938 and was named after Lt Col Horace M Hickam, an aviation pioneer who died in a crash in 1934 (*George Hall/Check Six*)

Left Good take-off photographs are rare, since the man with the camera is never sure where the rubber is going to leave the road. In this excellent 1990 study of one of the 199th's finest, an F-15A lifts off from Hickam AFB with the mountains of Oahu towering through the haze. Comparing this with the preceding photograph, the most striking difference is the toning-down of the Hawaiian ANG tail-marking. One may hope that the ending of the Cold War will bring back the colours of the 1980s
(*George Hall/Check Six*)

Below Two F-15As (84–0083 and friend) of the 199th FIS, ready to depart on an island patrol as a DC-9 comes in to Honolulu International in 1989. The 'Hawaii' tail-marking was surely one of the most decorative in the ANG
(*George Hall/Check Six*)

Below Two F-15As of the 199th head for the wild blue yonder in this 1990 shot, with undercarriages in different stages of retraction. At a weight of 50,000 lbs (22,700 kgs), the F-15A can take off with a ground roll of only 2500 ft (760 m), unsticking at 162 knots (300 km/hr). The standard-fit centreline tank is jettisonable (like the wing tanks carried for ferry flights), but produces some loss of stability (*George Hall/Check Six*)

Left The driver of the 199th's F-15A 74–0105 hits the burners of his F100-PW-100 turbofans and accelerates away. The optimum climb profile is obtained by starting at 350 knots (650 km/hr) and holding 0.95 IMN when that speed is reached, or 0.90 IMN without afterburner. The airframe limits are 800 knots (1480 km/hr) up to 41,000 ft (12,500 m), and then Mach 2.3, but brief excursions to Mach 2.5 are permitted (*George Hall/Check Six*)

Left The air superiority paint scheme of the
F-15 makes it a difficult aircraft to
photograph, but this tanker's view is about
as aesthetically pleasing as they come. The
Eagle in the picture is 74–0081, incidentally
the lowest number in the 199th's batch of
serials, and now well on the way to its 20th
birthday (*George Hall/Check Six*)

Strike Fighter

The Eagle has gone through several stages of development since the first F-15A took to the air on 27 July 1972, the 'one-holer' being followed by what was then known as the TF-15A two-seater on 7 July 1973. The two-seater was redesignated F-15B, and it was one such aircraft that became the first Eagle to be delivered to the USAF on 15 December 1974. Initial operational capability (IOC) was declared formally in July 1975 after 24 Eagles had been handed over to the service. Equipment of the first wing was completed by the end of 1976.

Production peaked at 144 aircraft per year, and in all 365 F-15As and 59 F-15Bs were manufactured. The second phase of development was the F-15C, which first flew on 27 February 1979, followed by the corresponding two-seat F-15D on 19 June 1979. These new aircraft differed from the F-15A/B mainly in having the capacity to carry an extra 2000 lbs (900 kgs) of internal fuel, programmable radar signal processors and provisions for two conformal fuel tanks which attach to the sides of the engine nacelles and house an additional 9750 lbs (4420 kgs) of fuel. These 'Fastpacks' incorporate hardpoints for external loads, and generate only a fraction of the additional drag created by three droptanks, which contain only 20 per cent more fuel.

Deliveries of the F-15C/D began in December 1981 to the 1st TFW at Langley AFB, Virginia, which is part of the Rapid Deployment Joint Task Force (RDJTF), and was one of the first units to be sent to Saudi Arabia during the 1990 crisis following the Iraqi invasion of Kuwait.

In order to exploit the Eagle's multi-role potential, McDonnell Aircraft took one of the early F-15Bs (serial 71–0291) and modified it for the ground attack role, using Fastpacks in combination with air-to-ground ordnance. Christened the Strike Eagle, the F-15E (as it became designated) first flew on 8 July 1980, and it was shown at Farnborough two months later, the company's objective being to secure USAF orders for this aircraft to supplement and later replace the F-111.

In 1982 the USAF identified the need for a new long-range interdiction aircraft, and two years later the service chose the F-15E for that role, in preference to the General Dynamics F-16XL. While retaining unsurpassed air superiority capabilities, the F-15E Eagle can penetrate deep into enemy territory by day and night regardless of weather conditions. It can strike high-value military targets such as roads, bridges and airfields with pinpoint accuracy. In addition to its Hughes APG-70 synthetic aperture radar, the

Right Line-up of F-15E dual-role fighters of the 336th TFS of the 4th TFW (tail-code 'SJ') at Seymour Johnson AFB in North Carolina, early in 1990. The 336th was the first operational unit to receive the F-15E, although crew training was carried out by the 461st TFTS ('Deadly Jesters') of the 405th TTW, and that wing's 550th TFTS now also has the 'Echo' version (*Mark Wagner*)

F-15E is equipped with Martin Marietta Lantirn (Low Altitude Navigation and Targeting Infra-Red for Night) pods, making possible safe low-level operation at night and in bad visibility without use of the main radar.

The first full-scale development (FSD) F-15E (serial 86–183) had its maiden flight on 11 December 1986, and on 29 December 1988 the first F-15E was delivered to the 336th TFS of the 4th TFW at Seymour Johnson AFB, North Carolina. Aircraft from this wing were deployed to Saudi Arabia in the Gulf War. Crew training for the F-15E is performed by the 461st and 550th TFTSs of the 405th TTW at Luke AFB, Arizona.

Below The much darker grey of the Eagle Echo gives it a far smarter appearance than the dedicated air superiority variants, though the choice of colour simply reflects the need to be able to operate at low level in the mud-moving role, making a difficult target for opposing pilots operating in a look-down visual search mode. This example (88–1670) carries the 4th TFW badge on the intake and the TAC insignia and the 336th's yellow stripe outlined in white on the fin (*Mark Wagner*)

Left A boomer's view of the F-15E, which carries conformally-mounted Fastpacks as standard, and in this instance has bombs attached to pylons on these tanks. Note also the use of only a single outrigger-pylon for the AIM-9M, although this is not standard on the F-15E. Each of the Dash-4 CFTs (conformal fuel tanks) can take up to six Mk 82 bombs weighing a nominal 500 lbs (227 kgs), but the maximum ordnance load (flight configuration 6) is 22 Mk 82s, of which six are carried on the centre-line, four on each CFT, and four on each of the inboard wing pylons. Maximum take-off weight is 81,000 lbs (36,740 kg) (*Mark Wagner*)

Above Closing in for a quick injection from a KC-10, this F-15E from the 336th TFS shows empty bomb-racks with the same old sway-bracing that US tactical fighters have traditionally dragged through the air. The F-15E begins life with the 23,770 lb (10,800 kg) F100-PW-220s, but in 1991 these engines are due to be uprated to PW-229 standard, while new-build aircraft will either have this or the F110-GE-129, both in the 29,000 lb (13,150 kg) class (*Mark Wagner*)

Right Fuel is now flowing from one McDonnell Douglas aircraft to another, although the F-15E was constructed at St Louis and the KC-10 at Long Beach. This look-down view emphasizes the long cockpit of the F-15E, a two-man crew having been specified for maximum effectiveness and safety in low level night operations. As one pilot with the F-15 Combined Test Force (CTF) at Edwards AFB said: 'The pilot rows the boat, and the WSO (weapon systems officer) shoots the

ducks.' The 4th TFW was one of the first units deployed to Saudi Arabia during the initial weeks of *Operation Desert Shield*. Based at Riyadh, the F-15Es received their baptism of fire alongside their single-seat brethren in the opening hours of *Desert Storm* on 17 January. Using their Lantirn system to great effect the crews of the 4th TFW wreaked havoc deep into Iraq, although several F-15Es were shot down by AAA (*Mark Wagner*)

Above left This remarkable photograph of the front cockpit of a fully-functioning F-15E shows the up-front controller (UFC) below the new Kaiser wide-angle holographic HUD, and below this a 5-inch (12.7 cm) multi-function colour display. On either side are 6-inch (15.2 cm) monochrome displays. In addition to weapon-aiming, the HUD can show all the usual flight information, and a FLIR picture of the outside world from the Lantirn pods. Each of the monochrome displays can show any of 18 different pictures, including a moving map, radar ground mapping, and FLIR images (*Mark Wagner*)

Below left The WSO's office features two 6-inch (15.2 cm) monochrome displays and two 5-inch (12.7 cm) units, of which one is monochrome and the other is coloured. A recorder system allows either split-screen or single-display formats. In addition, the rear cockpit has a keyboard and two hand controllers by which the WSO controls the displays (*Mark Wagner*)

Above Seen in silhouette, Capt Mike Stansbury and his personal F-15E of the 335th TFS, 4th TFW. Other users of Seymour Johnson AFB include SAC's KC-10-equipped 68th Air Refuelling Wing, the 916th Air Refuelling Group (AFRES) and elements of the 191st FIG of the Michigan ANG. The base was activated in 1942, and was named after US Navy Lt Seymour A Johnson, a native of the nearby city of Goldsboro who died in an aircraft accident in Maryland in the previous year (*Mark Wagner*)

Samurai Warrior

In 1975 the Japan Air Self-Defense Force (JASDF) began the task of selecting a fighter to complement the F-4EJ Phantom II in the all-weather air defence and air superiority roles. The JASDF philosophy was that the F-4EJ would not be capable of dealing with intruders flying either at a very high speed and altitude, or with aircraft penetrating at a very low level. Nor would the F-4EJ be able to deal with future Soviet fighters.

There were originally seven contenders, but these were soon reduced to the F-14, F-15 and F-16. The F-16 was then thrown out on the grounds of its relatively modest radar and ECM capability, the lack of space for future equipment growth and the performance reduction that would result when carrying the AIM-7 Sparrow medium-range air-to-air missile. The F-14 was judged to be outstanding in the air defence role, but its TF30 engines were felt to give it insufficient dogfight performance. In addition, the JASDF decided that the F-14 was undesirably complex and would require improvements to runway surfaces.

The elimination of the F-14 and F-16 left the F-15, and in December 1976 the Japan Defense Agency (JDA) informally adopted a policy of selecting the Eagle as the JASDF's follow-on fighter. In the event, discussions between the various ministries and agencies involved delayed the start of the procurement programme, and an extra 12 F-4EJs were purchased in FY77 as a stop-gap measure.

In April 1978 Mitsubishi was chosen to be prime contractor for the Eagle, which would be produced as the single-seat F-15J and two-seat F-15DJ, and for the AIM-7E Sparrow and AIM-9L Sidewinder that would arm it. The first two F-15Js and 12 F-15DJs were manufactured by McDonnell at St Louis. The

Left Two F-15J Eagles of the JASDF's 204 *Hikotai* of the 7th *Kokudan*, shown at Hyakuri AB, in company with some much paler F-4EJs. The eagle's head on the fin is the squadron badge. The national 'meatball' symbol (formally known as the Sun Disc) is not visible in this view, since it is painted on the front fuselage just ahead of the intakes. The JASDF serial number is based on a two-digit hyphenated combination indicating the aircraft type, with the second digit chosen according to its role. For example, –8 indicates an all-weather fighter, and 2–8 is the type-designator for an F-15J or the two-seat F-15DJ. The older F-4EJ has the type-designator 7–8. This two-digit designator is preceded by one digit indicating the year of delivery (not the year of purchase), fortunately on the Western calendar. It is followed by three digits giving the individual aircraft number, which is repeated on the nose. The two Eagles shown here (22–8805 and 12–8054) were thus delivered in 1982 and 1981 respectively, while the F-4EJ (47–8345) was delivered in 1974. The aircraft in the foreground was the fifth F-15J to be accepted, and the low serial of the second ('054) indicates that it is an F-15DJ. The first 12 two-seaters delivered to the JASDF were built at St Louis, and this was the fourth delivered, being a converted F-15D that previously bore the USAF serial 79–0285 (*Robbie Shaw*)

first F-15J was formally accepted by the JASDF at St Louis on 15 July 1980, and the two single-seaters (02–8801 and –8802) were flown to the Air Proving Wing at Gifu AB in March 1981. The first Mitsubishi-assembled F-15J (12–8803) flew on 26 August 1981 at Komaki, Nagoya.

The F-15J entered JASDF service in December 1981 with the *Rinji* F-15 *Hikotai* (Temporary F-15 Sqn) at Nyutabaru, on the southern island of Kyushu. One year later this unit was redesignated as 202 *Hikotai* of 5 *Kokudan* (Wing), which became the OCU and was also initially responsible for the Western Air Defense Sector. In April 1983 the first F-15Js were issued to 203 *Hikotai* of 2 *Kokudan* at Chitose on Hokkaido, covering the north of the country. A year later the third unit was formed, 204 *Hikotai* of 7 *Kokudan* at Hyakuri on the main island of Honshu covering the central region. This was followed by 201 *Hikotai* of 2 *Kokudan*, likewise at Chitose, and 303 and 205 *Hikotai* of 6 *Kokudan* at Komatsu in the central region. Western air defence now appears to be the responsibility of 304 and 306 *Hikotai* of 8 *Kokudan*, at Tsuiki AB on Kyushu.

It will be noted that from a JASDF viewpoint the air defense of Okinawa has been left to the F-4EJ, presumably because that island faces China, rather than Korea and the Soviet Union. However, Okinawa is defended by the only USAF Eagle unit in the Far East, the 18th TFW, based at Kadena AB.

Above This F-15J (72–8895) of the 202nd *Hikotai* of the 5th *Kokudan* was pictured landing at its base at Nyutabaru in 1990. This was the first squadron to be formed with the Eagle, and appears to be used primarily as an operational conversion unit (*Robbie Shaw*)

Right Close-up of F-15DJ '054 on the ramp at Hyakuri AB in early 1990. The angry eagle insignia and the dayglo-orange of the overalls are noteworthy (*Robbie Shaw*)

Its tail badge identifies this F-15DJ as belonging to the 202nd *Hikotai*, but it was photographed at nearby Komaki AB in 1987. Its serial (12–8052) tells us that it was the second two-seater to be delivered to Japan, the first having arrived on 6 April 1981. This second aircraft formerly bore the USAF serial 79–0283 (*Peter R Foster*)

An F-15J (82–8900) of the 202nd *Hikotai*, taxying at Nyutabaru in 1990. Its serial indicates that it was the 100th Eagle to be accepted by the JASDF, and was delivered in 1988. The F-15J is virtually identical to the USAF F-15C, right down to the camouflage scheme adopted, but it is believed to have a Japanese radar-warning receiver and a locally-developed ALQ-8 jamming pod (*Robbie Shaw*)

Above left A line-up of tails (including 92–8907, 22–8814 and 42–8834) belonging to F-15Js of the 304th *Hikotai* of 8 *Kokudan*, at its base at Tsuiki AB on the southern island of Kyushu, in 1990 (*Robbie Shaw*)

Left Eagles of the 304th *Hikotai* (including 72–8892, 52–8858, 52–8862, and 42–8843), providing an excellent example of an ideal target for cluster weapons. As seen at Tsuiki AB in 1990, they stand waiting for another Pearl Harbor, without a single hardened aircraft shelter in sight (*Robbie Shaw*)

Above The JASDF has its own version of the USAF's Aggressor squadrons, but it uses something more expensive than the F-5E or F-16. This F-15DJ (92–8068) is from the *Hiko Kyodotai*, which is based alongside the OCU at Nyutabaru. Note the squadron badge on the fin and the use of green and grey camouflage (*Robbie Shaw*)

Above The same aircraft in rear-quarter view. Perhaps surprisingly, neither the 'meatball' nor the overalls are toned down for air combat training (*Robbie Shaw*)

Above right The Americans have no monopoly on weird camouflage schemes, and this second F-15DJ (82–8065) from the aggressor unit at Nyutabaru appears to have a combination of pale grey and olive green that breaks up its visual shape, but can hardly make it difficult to spot (*Robbie Shaw*)

Right The world's most expensive aggressor aircraft taxies out at Nyutabaru. However, this is not the JASDF's only costly trainer. The Mitsubishi T-2 supersonic trainer (sometimes referred to as the 'Japanese Jaguar') was developed at a time when all other nations were building subsonic trainers for economy (*Robbie Shaw*)

Below This trio of PACAF Eagles hails from the 12th TFS of the 18th TFW (tail-code 'ZZ'), based at Kadena AB on Okinawa. The 18th is part of the 5th Air Force, headquartered at Yokota AB in Japan. The 5th AF also controls the 432nd TFW at Misawa AB in northern Honshu, currently equipped with F-16s. Kadena also accommodates SAC's 376th Strategic Wing, with KC-135s and RC-135s, and the 5th's 313th Air Division, which controls the 18th TFW, the 18th Combat Support Wing, and the 400th Munitions Maintenance Sqn (*Robbie Shaw*)

Left A handsome F-15C (78–0505) of the 12th TFS, over the endless expanse of the Pacific in 1986. The 18th TFW operates three squadrons, using an unusual system of tail-markings. As shown here, they have a triangular design instead of the usual stripe. The triangle has three colours, the predominant one indicating the squadron: yellow for the 12th TFS, blue for the 44th TFS, and red for the 67th TFS. Reports indicate that during 1990 the wing's aircraft were painted in a non-standard combination of greys, with serial number and tail-code in white (*Robbie Shaw*)

It has been a long night, and this F-15C of
the 44th TFS closes on the tanker at dawn
during a pre-ORI (Operational Readiness
Inspection) exercise in 1987 (*Peter R. Foster*)

Above An F-15C of the 44th TFS at Kadena in 1986. The predominant colour of the unit marking is supposedly blue, though in this picture it appears to be closer to black. Note the yellow receptacle cover, the PACAF insignia on the left fin, and the unit badge in the form of a samurai warrior's head. This aircraft (78–0494) is one of the earliest built F-15Cs, the first being 78–0468 (*Robbie Shaw*)

Above right This even earlier F-15C (78–0488) was photographed at Nellis AFB in 1982, just before being ferried to Okinawa. The predominant red of the triangular squadron marking identifies it as a member of the 67th TFS, but the three squadron badges on the intake suggests that this is the wing commander's aircraft (*US Official via Bob Archer*)

Below right An F-15C (78–0516) returns to Mother Earth in 1987, its tail marking denoting the 67th TFS. The nose leg carries separate lights for landing and taxying (*Robbie Shaw*)

Capt B Hoppe of the 67th TFS, portrayed giving his mount (78–0475) a drink somewhere over the Pacific in 1986 (*Robbie Shaw*)

The Desert Storm

Kuwait is a tiny, oil-rich state at the head of the Persian Gulf, wedged between the land-masses of Iraq and Saudi Arabia. As the various oil-producing areas of the world run dry, these three nations will assume growing importance, since their outputs will not begin to decline until the year 2100 in the case of Iraq and Saudi Arabia, and 2175 in the case of Kuwait. If Iraq were to be allowed to take over Kuwait, then it would become immensely powerful, and if it went on to gain control of Saudi oilfields, then within the foreseeable future Iraq would be able to directly control the price of oil.

From an Iraqi viewpoint, the conquest of Kuwait offered the immediate prospect of vastly increased oil revenues, and an avenue to move against Saudi (and other) oil facilities along the southern shore of the Gulf. It also offered the attraction of secure access to the Gulf for its own oil exports and other trade. As the basis for such a take-over, Iraq has long claimed that Kuwait is historically part of its Basra province.

On 2 August 1990 Iraq, incensed by Kuwait's excessive oil production depressing prices, and by Kuwait's refusal to write off the billions of dollars loaned to Iraq during the Gulf War with Iran, shocked the world by invading this tiny nation and gaining total control within a matter of hours.

Had this invasion occurred some years earlier, then the responsibility for Kuwait's defence would have rested firmly with Britain. Around the turn of the century, Britain reached a series of agreements with the smaller nations around the Gulf gaining basing facilities in exchange for external defence and various forms of assistance. In the case of Kuwait, the agreement dated from 1899, long before oil was discovered in the region. However, during the early postwar period Britain began pulling back its forces from the Middle East, arguing that nations such as Kuwait were now wealthy enough to pay for their own defence. In early June 1961 the agreement was thus replaced by a formal exchange of notes, in which Britain merely indicated a willingness to provide defence assistance if requested.

This change was perhaps misinterpreted in Iraq, which immediately renewed its claims and began moving forces toward the Kuwaiti border. On June 30th the Ruler asked for British assistance, and on July 1st British forces began pouring in from Bahrain and from the commando carrier *HMS Bulwark*. Hunter ground attack aircraft had been ferried in from Kenya and were based at Kuwait International, and tanks were landed from an LCT. By the 9th the carrier *HMS Victorious* had arrived from the Far East.

The Iraqi forces withdrew, and in due course the British forces were replaced by a small Arab League force. By 1971 UK forces were withdrawn

Right Close-up of Eagle 82–0009, showing the somewhat unusual air superiority camouflage scheme, which is quite different from that applied to 83–0010 (*Ian Black*)

from the Gulf, and the possibility of such rapid deployments was eliminated. From this point Kuwait had to defend itself and (if necessary) appeal for help to the United Nations.

Following Iraq's invasion on 2 August 1990, the UN called for an Iraqi withdrawal. Many nations sent forces to the area to deter any Iraqi move against the Saudi oilfields, and to prepare (if necessary) to drive Iraqi forces back across their border. America's *Operation Desert Shield* has been a deployment which has no equal, far exceeding the efforts made by any other country. Britain's own *Operation Granby* came a poor second.

The USAF deployment has involved many aircraft types, from the massive B-52 to the diminutive F-117A, but the first unit to deploy to Saudi Arabia was the 1st TFW, whose Eagles (given only 36 hours' notice to move out) began arriving at 10-minute intervals on August 8. By the end of that first day there were 25 F-15Cs on the ground at Bahrain, fuelled, armed and ready to take on any intruding Iraqi aircraft.

Within a short period all three squadrons were installed with 24 to 28 Eagles apiece and a total of about 3000 men. Day temperatures originally peaked at 123°F (50.5°C) and later soared to 135°F (57.2°C), but the F-15s of the 1st TFW went on providing their air umbrella, directed by the E-3s of the USAF and Royal Saudi Air Force.

Below Two F-15Cs of the 71st TFS, 1st TFW (83–0010 in the foreground, 82–0009 in the rear), photographed in a sunken 'flow-through' revetment at Dhahran AB in late 1990. An aircraft from this unit achieved the first aerial kill of the war on the opening night of *Desert Storm* (*Ian Black*)

Right Even in an advanced technology air battle, the time-worn sniper-scope has a role to play, at least in long-range target identification (*Ian Black*)

The air defence provided by the 1st TFW has supplemented that of the RSAF's own F-15C/Ds. At the start of August the RSAF had approximately 78 F-15Cs and 15 F-15Ds, which were almost immediately augmented by 12 from the 32nd TFS at Soesterberg and 12 from the 36th TFW at Bitburg. Saudi Eagles now equip No 13 and 42 Sqns at Dharan (King Abdul Aziz AB), No 5 Sqn at Taif (King Fahd AB) and No 6 Sqn at Kamis Mushayt (King Khaled AB).

After six months of relative quiet, the 1st TFW's F-15 force finally got to fly its first combat sorties on 17 January 1991 during the opening phase of *Operation Desert Storm*. Heavily involved in escorting Allied strike aircraft on sorties deep into enemy territory, the Eagles quickly drew first blood, a pilot from the 71st TFS claiming the first aerial kill of the war when he downed an Iraqi Mirage F.1 attempting to escape from an air base under attack. Numerous kills were then achieved by both US and Saudi 'Eagle drivers' over the following weeks as the Allied air forces systematically sanitized the skies over Iraq and Kuwait.

Right The squadron commander's aircraft (F-15C serial 82–0018) shows that the threat of war did not lead to a further toning-down of Eagle markings (*Ian Black*)

Above left The variation in paint-schemes is well-illustrated by this pair of 1st TFW Eagles at Dhahran. Traditionally, revetments have been built above ground for simplicity and low-cost, but this sunken design makes detection from low flying aircraft more difficult (*Ian Black*)

Above Another variation of the 1st TFW's camouflage and another type of accommodation. Maintenance work appears to be performed in these airy shelters, but there are also hardened aircraft shelters available at Dhahran. The tail marking suggests that this is the wing commander's personal aircraft (*Ian Black*)

This smart F-15C carries the words 'Royal
Saudi Air Force' and its aerial '1312' in both
English script and what is known
irreverently as 'wormspeak'. The unit
badge is also painted on the fin, but it is not
clear whether this relates to No 13 Sqn or
No 42 (*Ian Black*)

Close-up of the front fuselage, which must have been a nightmare for the paint-shop at St Louis (*Ian Black*)

Above An engine-change for Saudi F-15C serial 1315 illustrating horizontal extraction, which requires far more floor area than the vertical change used on (for example) the F/A-18 (*Ian Black*)

Above right A Saudi F-15C in a hangar at Dhahran, undergoing a 100-hour maintenance check. As with their USAF brothers, Saudi pilots were heavily involved in performing CAP patrols over Iraq and Kuwait during the opening phase of *Desert Storm*. On one of these sorties a Saudi pilot managed to down two MiG-23s escorting Exocet-equipped Mirage F.1s (*Ian Black*)

Below right As the sign indicates, this aircraft is jacked up to allow maintenance and hydraulic checks to be carried out. Equipment commonality between the RSAF and USAF on the Eagle (and between the RSAF and RAF on Tornado) was a major factor in enhancing the operational efficiency of the air forces gathered to eject Iraq from Kuwait (*Ian Black*)

A further view of this maintenance facility
at King Abdul Aziz AB, Dhahran. The two
red triangles on the aircraft in the
foreground indicate that this is an F-15D
(*Ian Black*)